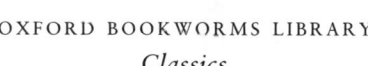

OXFORD BOOKWORMS LIBRARY
Classics

The Wind in the Willows

Stage 3 (1000 headwords)

W0018936

Series Editor: Jennifer Bassett
Founder Editor: Tricia Hedge
Activities Editors: Jennifer Bassett and Christine Lindop

KENNETH GRAHAME

The Wind in the Willows

Retold by
Jennifer Bassett

Illustrated by
Jan McCafferty

OXFORD UNIVERSITY PRESS

OXFORD
UNIVERSITY PRESS

Great Clarendon Street, Oxford OX2 6DP

Oxford University Press is a department of the University of Oxford.
It furthers the University's objective of excellence in research, scholarship,
and education by publishing worldwide in

Oxford New York

Auckland Cape Town Dar es Salaam Hong Kong Karachi
Kuala Lumpur Madrid Melbourne Mexico City Nairobi
New Delhi Shanghai Taipei Toronto

With offices in

Argentina Austria Brazil Chile Czech Republic France Greece
Guatemala Hungary Italy Japan Poland Portugal Singapore
South Korea Switzerland Thailand Turkey Ukraine Vietnam

OXFORD and OXFORD ENGLISH are registered trade marks of
Oxford University Press in the UK and in certain other countries

This simplified edition © Oxford University Press 2008
Database right Oxford University Press (maker)
First published in Oxford Bookworms 1995

8 10 9

ISBN 978 0 19 479137 3

Printed in China

Word count (main text): 11,540 words

For more information on the Oxford Bookworms Library,
visit www.oup.com/bookworms

CONTENTS

1

The river

The Mole worked very hard all morning, cleaning his little home. He brushed, and he washed; he cleaned the floors and the walls, he stood on chairs to wash the tops of cupboards, he got under the beds, he took up the carpets. He cleaned and he cleaned, until his arms and his back ached with tiredness.

It was springtime, and the smell and the sound of spring were everywhere, even in the Mole's dark little house under the ground. And with the spring comes the promise of change, of sunshine, of new green leaves. So it was not surprising that the Mole suddenly put down his brushes and said, 'Oh bother!' and then, 'I'm tired of cleaning!' Something up above the ground was calling to him, and he ran out of his house and began to dig his way upwards to the sun.

The Mole suddenly put down his brushes.

1

He dug and he pushed, and he pushed and he dug. 'Up we go! Up we go!' he said to himself, until at last his nose came out into the sunlight, and he found himself in the warm grass of a field.

'This is fine!' said the Mole. 'This is better than cleaning!' The sunshine was warm on his back and the air was filled with the songs of birds. He gave a little jump for happiness, shook himself, and then began to cross the field towards some trees. Here and there he went, through the fields and the woods, looking and smelling and listening. Everywhere animals and birds were busy, talking and laughing, looking for food, making new homes for the spring. The Mole enjoyed it all.

Then, suddenly, he came to a river. He had never seen a river before in his life – this wonderful bright shining thing, which danced its way in and out of the shadows under the trees. It was never still for a minute, hurrying and laughing and talking to itself.

And at once, the Mole was in love with it. He walked along the river bank, listening and watching all the time. At last he sat down on the grass and looked across the river to the bank opposite. There was a dark hole in the bank, and the Mole watched it dreamily, thinking that it would be very pleasant to have a little house by the river. As he watched, he saw something shining in the hole. Soon he saw that it was an eye, and then a face appeared as well.

A brown little face, with whiskers.

With bright eyes, and small ears, and thick shiny hair.

It was the Water Rat!

It was the Water Rat!

Then the two animals stood up and looked at each other.

'Hello, Mole!' said the Water Rat.

'Hello, Rat!' said the Mole.

'Would you like to come over?' asked the Rat.

'Oh, it's easy to *talk*,' said the Mole, a little crossly. The river was new to him and he did not know how to get to the other side.

The Rat said nothing, and disappeared. Then he appeared again, in a little blue and white boat, which came quickly across the river towards the Mole. It stopped by the bank, and a moment later the Mole, to his great surprise and excitement, found himself actually sitting in a real boat.

3

'Do you know,' he said, as the Rat began to row away from the bank, 'I've never been in a boat before in all my life.'

'What?' cried the Rat. 'My dear fellow, you haven't lived! Believe me,' he went on seriously, 'there is *nothing* – really nothing – nicer than just messing about in boats. You can go up river, down river, stay where you are, it really doesn't matter. There's always something to do, but you don't have to do it if you don't want to. You can do what you like. Look here! If you're not busy today, why don't we spend the day on the river together?'

The Mole had listened to all this with great interest. Now he sat back in the comfortable seat and said, 'What a wonderful day this is! Let's start at once!'

But first the Rat went into his hole, and after a while came out carrying a very large and heavy lunch basket. This went into the boat, under the Mole's feet, and then the Rat began to row down river. The two friends talked from time to time, but mostly the Mole just watched the river dreamily, enjoying the sounds and the smells and the sunlight. At last they turned off the big river into a little side river that came down to join it. The Rat stopped the boat and they got out on to a bank of soft green grass under tall willow trees. It was very quiet and very peaceful.

The Mole sat down and looked around him. 'What a beautiful place!' he said happily.

'Time for lunch,' said the Rat, opening the basket. 'Come on, Mole! Let's get to work.'

The Mole was happy to obey, because he was very hungry

4

indeed after all his cleaning earlier in the day. And what a
lunch it was! There were cold meats and egg sandwiches,
cooked chicken and tomatoes, apples and bananas and a large
cake.

'Time for lunch,' said the Rat.

When at last they could eat no more, the Mole lay back and watched the river lazily. After a while he sat up.

'I can see a long line of bubbles in the water,' he said. 'I wonder what it is.'

'I can see a long line of bubbles in the water.'

'Bubbles? Oho!' said the Rat, and he called out across the river in a friendly kind of way.

The bubbles stopped and turned. Soon a wet whiskery nose appeared above the edge of the bank, and the Otter pulled himself out and shook the water from his coat.

'A lunch party!' he said, going straight towards the food. 'Why didn't you invite me, Ratty?'

'We didn't plan it,' explained the Rat. 'We only decided to come this morning. Oh, and this is my friend, Mr Mole.'

'Happy to meet you,' said the Otter, and the two animals were friends at once.

'All the world seems to be out on the river today,' said the Otter while he ate. 'I came up this side river to try and get a moment's peace, and then I find you fellows having a lunch party!'

Suddenly there was a noise in the thick bushes behind them, and a big black and white head looked out at them.

'Come on, old Badger!' shouted the Rat.

The Badger came forward a few steps, then stopped. 'Hmm! A crowd!' he said crossly, and turned his back and disappeared again into the bushes.

'What a pity!' said the Rat. 'Dear old Badger! He's a good fellow, but he does hate a crowd. We won't see him again today. But tell us, *who*'s out on the river?'

'Toad's out, for one,' replied the Otter. 'In his shiny new boat. He's got new boating clothes, and everything!'

The Rat and the Otter looked at each other and laughed.

'Toad's always trying something new,' the Rat explained to the Mole. 'But

The Badger came forward a few steps.

he always gets bored so quickly. Last year it was a house-boat, and he wanted to spend the rest of his life living on the river. This year it's rowing-boats.'

'He's a nice fellow, of course,' said the Otter. 'But he never learns from his mistakes!'

From where they sat they could see a bit of the big river. And just then they saw a rowing-boat going past, and in it a short fat animal, rowing very hard and very badly.

'There's Toad going past now,' said the Rat. 'Look at him! He'll turn that boat over in a minute.'

'Of course he will,' laughed the Otter. Toad had now disappeared up river, and the Otter went on, 'Did I ever tell you that story about Toad and the . . .'

There was a sudden movement in the water near the bank. Something silvery shone for a second, then it was gone. And so was the Otter. The Mole looked down. The Otter's voice was still in his ears, but the Otter had disappeared.

There was just a long line of bubbles in the river.

The Rat sang a little song to himself, and the Mole remembered that it was not at all polite, in the animal world, to say anything if your friends disappeared at any moment, for any reason.

'Well, well,' said the Rat. 'I suppose we should think about getting home.'

The Mole packed the things away in the lunch basket, and soon the Rat began to row gently homewards while the afternoon sun went down behind the trees. The Rat was dreaming quietly to himself, but the Mole was very full of lunch and the excitements of the day. He began to think that he knew everything about boats now.

And in a while he said, 'Ratty! Please, *I* want to row!'

The Rat shook his head with a smile. 'Not yet, my young friend,' he said. 'Wait until you've had a few lessons. It's not as easy as it looks.'

The Mole was quiet for a minute or two. But he wanted to row very much indeed. He was sure that he could row as well as Rat. Then, before the Rat could stop him, he jumped up, and pulled the oars out of the surprised Rat's hands. The Rat fell backwards off his seat, calling out, 'Stop it, you silly fellow! You'll have us in the river!'

The Mole made a great dig at the water with the oars, but the oars never touched the water at all. The Mole's legs flew up above his head, and he found himself lying on top of the Rat in the bottom of the boat. Frightened, he tried to get up, got hold of the side of the boat, and the next moment – splash!

The oars never touched the water at all.

9

Over went the boat, and the Mole and the Rat and the lunch basket were all in the water.

It was the Rat, of course, who pulled the Mole out of the water, who turned the boat right way up, who found the oars, who got the lunch basket from the bottom of the river. And he laughed and laughed.

When all was ready again, the unhappy Mole sat in the boat, very wet and very miserable. As they left, he said in a low voice, 'Ratty, my dear friend! I have been so silly and so ungrateful. I really am very sorry indeed.'

'That's all right!' replied the Rat kindly. 'I'm always in and out of the water myself, so don't worry about it. But I really think you should come and stay with me for a while. You'll be very comfortable, and I'll teach you to row and to swim. Soon you'll be as good a boatman as any of us.'

The Mole was almost too happy to speak and could find no words to thank his friend.

When they got home, they had a good hot supper in front of a bright fire while the Rat told exciting stories of life on the river. Then he took the Mole upstairs to the best bedroom, and soon the Mole was lying warm and comfortable, listening to the sound of his new friend the River running past his bedroom window.

That was the first of many wonderful days for the Mole, as the spring turned slowly into a golden summer. He learnt to swim and to row, and he learnt to love the sound of the wind when it went whispering its secrets through the trees and the plants by the river.

2

The open road

One bright summer morning the Mole and the Rat were out on the river bank, watching the world go by. The Rat was writing a song and was singing quietly to himself as he tried different words.

'Ratty,' said the Mole, 'could I ask you something?'

'Mmm,' the Rat said, not really listening. 'Sky, fly, high, die, why . . . Oh dear! What did you say, Mole?'

'Will you take me to visit Mr Toad? I've heard so much about him, and I do want to meet him.'

'Why, of course,' said the Rat kindly. 'Get the boat out, and we'll row up there now. Toad's always happy to see his friends.'

'He must be a very nice animal,' said the Mole, as he got into the boat and took the oars.

'He's the best of animals,' replied the Rat. 'Kind, friendly – not very clever, perhaps, and sometimes he's just a little bit boastful, but he's a good fellow really.'

The Mole rowed hard up the river and in a while they came to a large red house, with beautiful gardens reaching down to the water's edge.

'There's Toad Hall,' said the Rat. 'It's a lovely old house – Toad is very rich, you know, and this is really one of the nicest houses on the river. But we never say that to Toad, of course.'

They left their boat by the boathouse at the end of the

garden. The boathouse was full of expensive boats, which looked new and mostly unused.

The Rat looked around him. 'I see that all the boats are out of the water,' he said. 'I suppose Toad has finished with boating now and has some new interest to amuse him.'

They walked over the grass towards the house and soon found Toad, resting in a garden-chair and carefully studying a large map.

'Wonderful!' he cried, as he saw them. 'You're just the fellow that I wanted to see, Ratty.' He jumped up and came towards them, talking all the time, and gave the Rat no time to introduce the Mole. 'I need you very much – both of you. You've got to help me. It's most important!'

'It's about your rowing, I suppose,' said the Rat, keeping his face very serious. 'You *will* learn to do it in the end, you know, if you're patient and work hard and— '

'Oh, bother boats!' the Toad said crossly. 'I've finished with boats. Silly way to pass the time. No, I've discovered the real thing – the best way, the *only* way, to spend one's life. Come with me, dear Ratty, and your kind friend too, and I will show you!'

He took them round to the other side of the house, and there they saw a shiny new gipsy caravan. It had yellow and green sides, and red wheels.

'There you are!' cried the Toad. 'There's real life for you. The open road, the fields, the hills . . . villages, towns, cities! Here today, off to a different place tomorrow! Travel, change, interest – the world in front of you!'

They saw a shiny new gipsy caravan.

The Mole was very interested and excited, and followed the Toad inside the caravan to look around. But the Rat shook his head and waited outside.

When they came down the steps again, the Toad was still talking excitedly to the Mole. 'So you see, everything is ready for when we start this afternoon.'

'What was that?' said the Rat slowly. 'Did you say "we" and "start" and "this afternoon"?'

'Now, dear good old Ratty,' said Toad quickly, 'don't talk in that cross voice. You know you've *got* to come. You can't

13

stay by your boring old river all your life. I want to show you the world!'

'I don't care,' said the Rat calmly. 'I'm not coming, and that's final. I'm going to stay by my old river, and what's more, Mole's going to stay with me, aren't you, Mole?'

'Of course I am,' said the Mole bravely. But his face looked sad. Poor Mole! He thought that life in a caravan on the open road would be an exciting adventure.

The Rat saw his sad face and felt worried. He liked his friends to be happy and he could see that the Mole really wanted to go.

Toad watched them both carefully. 'Come in and have some lunch,' he said pleasantly, 'and we'll talk it over.'

During lunch – which was excellent, of course, because everything at Toad Hall always was – the Toad talked and talked. He was full of wonderful plans. How interesting each day would be! What adventures the three friends would have together! Ah, the happiness of the travelling life!

In the end, of course, the Rat agreed to go, and by the evening they found themselves on a lonely hillside miles from home. It had been a golden afternoon, and even the Rat had enjoyed the journey so far. Only the old grey horse was not very happy. He had to do all the hard work of pulling the caravan, and he was not at all pleased about it.

The next morning the Toad was still sleeping deeply when the other two got up. They shook him very hard but couldn't wake him, so they had to do all the work. The Rat took care of the horse, lit the fire, and did last night's washing-up. The Mole walked to the nearest village, a long way away, to get milk and eggs and bread, which the Toad had, of course, forgotten to bring. And when at last the Toad got up, he said what a pleasant easy life it was on the open road.

The day passed happily as they travelled over green hills and along narrow country roads. But the next morning the Rat and the Mole got Toad out of bed and made sure that he did some of the work. Because of this, Toad said very little about a pleasant easy life. Later, he even tried to get back into bed, but the Mole and the Rat pulled him out again.

The end of their journey came very suddenly. In the afternoon they were travelling along a big road. The Mole was walking beside the horse, and the Toad and the Water Rat were walking behind the caravan, talking together. Actually, the Toad was talking, and the Rat was listening – some of the time.

Then they heard a noise behind them, and looking back, they saw a small cloud of dust. It made a 'Poop-poop!' sound, and it was coming towards them very fast indeed.

Looking back, they saw a small cloud of dust.

15

Seconds later, the peace of the afternoon was destroyed in a storm of noise and wind and dust. The 'poop-poop' rang with a shout in their ears, and an enormous, long, shining motor-car roared past them and disappeared over the hill.

The old grey horse, wild with fear, tried to get off the road. The caravan's wheels began to go down into the ditch along the edge. Then there was a terrible crash – and the beautiful yellow and green caravan lay helplessly on its side.

The Rat jumped up and down in the road, shouting angrily. 'Stupid, dangerous people! The police should lock you up in prison!'

The beautiful caravan lay helplessly on its side in the ditch.

He and the Mole managed to calm the horse, and then they went to look at the caravan. Two wheels had come off, the windows were broken, and bits of wood lay everywhere. They tried to pull it out of the ditch, but they couldn't move it.

'Hi! Toad!' they cried. 'Come and help us, can't you!'

The Toad never answered a word, so they went to see what was the matter with him. They found him sitting in the middle of the road, with a dreamy smile on his face and happily whispering, 'Poop-poop!'

The Rat shook him, not very gently. 'Are you coming to help us, Toad?' he asked crossly.

'Oh, what happiness!' whispered Toad to himself. 'The *real* way to travel! The *only* way to travel! Here one minute – miles away in seconds! Wonderful! Poop-poop!'

'Oh, do stop being so silly, Toad!' cried the Mole.

'And I never *knew*!' the Toad went on dreamily. 'I never *dreamt*! What clouds of dust will fly up behind me as I drive like the wind! I've finished with silly old caravans for ever. Poop-poop!'

'What are we going to do with him?' the Mole asked the Water Rat.

'Nothing,' replied the Rat. 'There's nothing that we can do. I know Toad. When he gets a new idea into his head, he always goes crazy at first. He'll be like this for some days now. Come on, we'll have to do everything by ourselves.'

They had to leave the caravan in the ditch and walk to the nearest town, five or six miles away. There they asked somebody to take care of the horse, and found somebody who agreed to fetch the broken caravan. Then they caught a train to a station near Toad Hall, took Toad home, went down to the boat, and then at last they sat down to a late supper in Rat's comfortable little home by the river.

The next day was a lazy one. In the evening the Mole was sitting on the river bank fishing, when the Rat, who had been to visit friends, came to find him.

'Heard the news?' the Rat said. 'Everybody's talking about it, all along the river bank. Toad went up to town by an early train this morning. And he has ordered a large and very expensive motor-car.'

3

The Wild Wood

The Mole had wanted for a long time to meet the Badger. He often spoke about his wish to the Water Rat, but the Rat didn't seem to want to do anything about it.

'It's all right,' the Rat always said. 'Badger will come past one day, and then I'll introduce you.'

'Couldn't you invite him to dinner or something?' asked the Mole.

'He wouldn't come,' said the Rat. 'He hates crowds, and parties, and dinners, and all that kind of thing.'

'Well then, shall we go and visit *him*?'

'Oh, no!' the Rat said. 'He's very shy, and he wouldn't like that at all. I know him very well, but I've *never* visited his home. And it's not really possible to go there, because he lives right in the middle of the Wild Wood.'

'You said you would tell me about the Wild Wood,' said the Mole, 'but you never did. Aren't they – aren't they very nice people in there?'

'Well,' said the Rat, 'the squirrels are all right, and the rabbits – most of them. And Badger, of course. He *likes* living there. And nobody gives *him* any trouble.'

'But who *could* give trouble?' asked the Mole.

'There are, well, others,' the Rat went on slowly. 'Weasels ... stoats ... ferrets, and so on. They're all right in a way. Most of the time. But, well, you wouldn't want to turn your back to them in the dark, and that's a fact. Don't worry about Badger. He'll come along one day.'

But the summer passed and the Badger never came along.

'The squirrels are all right, and the rabbits.'

'There are, well, others ... weasels ... stoats ... ferrets.'

Soon the days grew shorter, and the cold weather kept the animals inside their comfortable houses. The Rat slept a lot in the winter, going to bed early and getting up late. During his short day, he wrote songs and did small jobs in the house. And, of course, there were always animals calling in for a comfortable talk round the fire, telling stories and remembering the good times and the adventures of the past summer.

One afternoon, while the Rat was sleeping peacefully in front of the fire, the Mole decided to go out by himself and take a walk in the Wild Wood. 'Perhaps,' he thought, 'I'll meet Mr Badger, and then I can introduce myself.'

It was a cold afternoon, with a hard grey sky. The Mole hurried along, enjoying the quietness of the winter day, and after a time he saw in front of him the black shape of the Wild Wood.

He was not at all frightened at first. It was a strange, dark place, but the Mole found that exciting. He went deeper and deeper into the wood, where the light was less and the trees grew close together. Everything was very still now, and the darkness seemed to come down quickly, shutting the Mole off from the outside world.

Then the faces began.

Out of the corner of his eye, the Mole thought that he saw a face looking at him from a hole: a little narrow face, with hard unfriendly eyes. When he turned to look straight at it, the thing had disappeared.

He hurried on, telling himself not to be silly. He passed another hole, and another, and – yes! Eyes were looking at him, then disappearing again into the darkness. Soon, every hole had a face, which watched him with eyes full of hate.

The Mole felt he had to get away from these faces. He turned off the path and hurried into the thickest part of the wood.

Then the whistling began.

It was soft, and far behind him, when he first heard it. Then it seemed to come from in front of him, more loudly. The Mole stopped and listened, then went on again. He was trying hard to stay calm, but his heart was beating very fast. He was alone, and far from help, and the night was coming down quickly.

Then the pattering began.

At first he thought it was only falling leaves, but then the noise grew louder and nearer, and the Mole knew what it was. It was the sound of little feet running – behind him, in front of him, on all sides of him. All the wood seemed to be alive,

*The Mole turned off the path and hurried into
the thickest part of the wood.*

running, following, chasing something – or somebody. The
frightened Mole began to run too, but he did not know where.
He ran into trees and bushes, he fell over things and into
things, he picked himself up and ran on. At last he found a deep
dark hole in the bottom of an old tree and fell into it, too tired
to run another step. He lay there, shaking with fear, and
listened to the whistlings and the patterings outside. Now he
understood why the Rat did not want to talk about it, and why
other small animals from the fields and the river bank never
came here. Because now, the Mole had felt it himself – the
Terror of the Wild Wood.

All this time the Rat, warm and comfortable, was sleeping in front of his fire. When he woke up, he looked round for his friend, but the Mole was not there. He called out 'Moly!' several times, and when he heard no answer, he got up and went out into the hall.

The Mole's hat was missing, and so were his boots.

The Rat left the house and looked around. The ground was soft from rain, and he could see clearly which way the Mole had gone – straight towards the Wild Wood.

The Rat stood thinking for a moment, looking very serious. Then he went back into the house, took a gun and a thick heavy stick, and hurried away across the fields.

Inside the wood it was nearly dark, and the whistling and the pattering began almost at once. But when the faces in the holes saw the Rat's gun and his thick heavy stick, they disappeared immediately, and everything became still and quiet. Patiently, the Rat began to search the wood from end to end, calling all the time, 'Moly, Moly! Where are you? It's me – it's old Rat!'

At last, to his great happiness, he heard a little answering cry, and soon he found the Mole in his hiding-place in the tree.

'Oh, Ratty!' cried the Mole. 'I'm so pleased to see you! I've been so frightened, I can't tell you!'

'I can understand that,' said the Rat kindly. 'You see, Mole, it's really not a good idea to come here alone. We river-bankers always come in twos or threes, if we have to come here. Of course, if you're Badger or Otter, then there's no problem.'

'Surely the brave Mr Toad is happy to come here alone, isn't he?' asked the Mole.

'Old Toad?' said the Rat, laughing loudly. 'He doesn't put his nose inside the Wild Wood – much too frightened!'

The Mole felt a little happier when he heard this, but he was still too tired to start the journey home. So he lay down to sleep under some dry leaves, while the Rat sat next to him, patiently waiting.

The Mole woke up feeling much better, and ready to leave. The Rat put his head out of the entrance of the hole, and then the Mole heard him say, 'Oh dear, oh dear!'

'What's the matter, Ratty?' asked the Mole.

'Snow,' replied the Rat. 'It's snowing hard. But we can't stay here all night – it's too cold, and too dangerous. We'll just have to start walking, and hope. The trouble is, I don't really know where we are, and in the snow everything looks so different.'

It did indeed. The white blanket of snow covered everything, hiding the paths, changing the shapes of the trees and bushes. An hour later, they were wet, cold, aching with tiredness, and had no idea where they were.

They sat down for a rest and were moving on again when the Mole gave a sudden cry and fell forward on his face.

'Oh, my leg!' he cried. 'I've hit my leg on something really hard.'

'Let's have a look,' said the Rat, sitting down beside him. 'That's a very deep cut,' he said, surprised. 'I wonder what . . .' Suddenly, he got up and began to dig in the snow.

'What *are* you doing, Ratty?' said the Mole.

The Rat just went on digging. Then he found something, and immediately began to dance round it excitedly.

'Look at this, Mole!' he shouted. 'Just look at this!'

The Mole looked. Then he looked at his friend. 'It's a door-scraper. Why get excited about a door-scraper?'

'Don't you understand, you silly animal?' cried the Rat.

'I understand that somebody's been very careless, leaving a door-scraper lying in the middle of the Wild Wood, for other people to fall over. And when I get home—'

'It's a door-scraper.'

'Oh dear, oh dear!' cried the Rat. 'Just stop arguing, and dig! Or do you want to spend all night in the snow?'

The Mole did what he was told, although he thought his friend was going crazy. The two animals dug and dug, and after ten minutes' hard work they were successful.

The Mole had thought that they were digging into a snow-bank, but now he saw that there was a door under the snow. A green door, with a long bell-pull beside it, and a name on it in big letters which said:

MR BADGER

The Mole fell backwards on the snow in surprise. 'Oh, Rat!' he cried. 'How clever you are! And how stupid I am!'

'Never mind all that,' said the Rat. 'Just get up and pull on that bell, while I knock on the door.'

The Rat banged on the door with his stick, and the Mole pulled. And from somewhere far under the ground they could just hear the sound of a deep, slow bell.

The Rat banged, and the Mole pulled.

4

A meeting with Mr Badger

They waited patiently for a very long time, jumping up and down in the snow to keep warm. At last they heard feet coming slowly towards the door. Then the door opened, just enough to show a long nose and pair of sleepy eyes.

'And who,' said a deep, angry voice, 'is making visits at this time of night?'

'Oh, Badger,' cried the Rat, 'let us in, please. It's me, Rat, and my friend Mole, and we're lost in the snow.'

'What?' said the Badger, in a very different voice. 'My dear Ratty! Lost in the snow, and in the Wild Wood! Come in at once, both of you, and get yourselves warm.'

That was a wonderful moment for the Mole and the Rat, when they heard the door close *behind* them, shutting out the Wild Wood. They followed the Badger down long dark tunnels until they came into a large kitchen. There was a bright fire, with comfortable armchairs round it, and a great wooden table with long seats.

'This is not the kind of night for small animals to be out,' the Badger said, in a fatherly way. 'Sit yourselves down by the fire, while I get you some supper.'

Soon the Mole and the Rat were warm and dry, and the dangers of the Wild Wood seemed a long way away, like a bad dream. Then supper arrived. It was enough for ten small hungry animals, and the Rat and the Mole realized just how

They followed the Badger down long dark tunnels.

hungry they were. When at last they could eat no more, they sat with the Badger round the fire, and told him the story of their adventures.

Then the Badger said, 'Now then! Tell me the news from your part of the world. How's old Toad getting on?'

'He's going from bad to worse,' said the Rat sadly. 'He had another crash only last week, and a bad one. You see, *he* thinks

28

he's a wonderful driver, the best in the world. But he isn't. He's terrible! But he won't take lessons, he won't listen to anyone.'

'How many has he had?' the Badger asked.

'Crashes, or motor-cars?' asked the Rat. 'Well, with Toad, it's the same thing. This is the seventh car, and the seventh crash. His garage is full to the roof with bits of broken motor-car!'

'He's been in hospital twice,' the Mole added. 'The police have arrested him for dangerous driving three or four times. And he's spending so much money!'

'That's another problem,' the Rat went on. 'Toad's rich, we all know that; but his money won't last for ever. Sooner or later, one of two things will happen. He'll kill himself in a crash, or he'll have no money left at all. Badger! We're his friends – can't we do something?'

The Badger thought for a while. 'You know, don't you, that I can't do anything *now*?' he said at last.

'No, no, of course not,' the Rat and the Mole said together. Everybody knew that in the animal world the winter was a time for rest and sleep. Nobody wanted to do anything important or tiring.

'Very well,' continued the Badger. 'But when the days are longer and warmer, then we'll do something. We – you and me and our friend the Mole here – we'll try to teach Toad a lesson. We won't listen to any silliness. We'll bring him back to reason, and turn him into a sensible Toad at last. But now, it's time for bed. Don't hurry tomorrow morning – come for breakfast as late as you want!'

29

The two tired animals slept long and deeply, and came down to breakfast very late indeed. In the kitchen they found two young hedgehogs, busy with bowls of bread and hot milk.

'Hello!' said the Rat pleasantly. 'Where did you two come from? Lost your way in the snow, I suppose?'

'Yes, sir,' said one of the hedgehogs politely. 'We got lost on the way to school, and Mr Badger said we could come in and have some breakfast.'

The breakfast things were all ready on the table, and the Mole and the Rat quickly got to work. The Rat made the coffee while the Mole fried several pieces of bread and an enormous number of eggs.

When the door bell rang, one of the hedgehogs went to

The hedgehog came back followed by the Otter.

30

answer the door. He came back followed by the Otter, who gave a shout of happiness when he saw the Rat. He ran across the room and almost knocked the Rat off his chair.

'Get off!' said the Rat, with his mouth full of fried bread.

'I thought I'd find you here all right,' said the Otter happily. 'Everybody along the river bank has been so worried about you. Rat never came home last night, and nor did Mole; something terrible has happened, they said. But if anyone's in trouble, Badger usually gets to hear about it, so I came straight here this morning. And oh my, didn't the Wild Wood look grand, with the snow everywhere and the red sun coming up, shining through the black trees! Halfway here I met one of those silly rabbits. He told me that Mole had lost his way last

night, and that "They" were out and chasing him all over the wood. I'd like to meet one of "Them" myself this morning, and tell them what I think.'

'Weren't you at all – um – afraid?' asked the Mole, remembering how frightened *he* had been.

'Afraid?' The Otter laughed and showed his strong white teeth. 'I don't think any of them would argue with *me*. Here, Mole, be a good fellow and fry me some eggs. I'm terribly hungry, and I've got a lot to talk about with Ratty here. Haven't seen him for weeks.'

Breakfast was almost finished when the Badger entered, looking sleepy. 'It's nearly time for lunch,' he said. 'Stay and have some with us, Otter. You must be hungry this cold morning.'

The hedgehogs were sent home, the breakfast things were cleared away, and soon the four animals sat down to lunch together. The Rat and the Otter were having a long conversation about river-bank matters, so the Mole began to talk to the Badger.

'This is a wonderful, comfortable home you have here,' he said. 'There's really nothing better than a place underground like this. You can shut off the world up there when you don't want it. And when you do, you can just go up and there's the world waiting for you.'

The Badger smiled warmly at him. 'That's just what I say,' he replied. 'Down here, you're safe and dry and warm. With a house above ground, you've got to worry about fire, and wind and rain, holes in the roof and broken windows. No, above ground is fine in its way, but one's *home* should be underground.'

The Mole agreed with everything that the Badger said. His own little home was underground, so it was natural for him to feel comfortable there. He and the Badger became very friendly, and after lunch the Badger took him all round his home, down tunnel after tunnel, through room after room. The Mole was interested in everything and thought it was all wonderful.

When they got back to the kitchen, the Rat was walking up and down, very restless. Unlike the Mole, he didn't really feel comfortable underground. He wanted to be back in his own home, where the windows looked out over the river, and where he could hear the wind whispering through the trees.

'Come along, Mole,' he said. 'We must get off while it's daylight. We don't want to spend another night lost in the Wild Wood.'

'It's all right,' said the Otter. 'I'm coming with you and I know all the paths.'

'You mustn't worry, Ratty,' added the Badger calmly. 'My tunnels go further than you think, and I've several back doors at the edge of the wood – although I keep them secret from most people.'

So the journey home was really very easy. When they came out of the Badger's secret back door, they found a path across the fields and soon they could see the river in front of them. The Mole looked back at the Wild Wood for a moment, thinking

The Mole looked back at the Wild Wood.

of the terror that he had felt there. Then he hurried on after the others, happy to be back in the open fields, and looking forward to the bright firelight of home.

A lesson for Mr Toad

Winter passed, and spring returned to the river bank. Then came a fine morning in early summer, when the world seemed full of sunlight and new green leaves. Down by the river bank, the Mole and the Water Rat were hard at work, mending and cleaning boats, looking for lost oars, and getting ready for a summer on the river. Then they went in to breakfast and had nearly finished when they heard a heavy knock on the door.

The Mole went to see who it was, and came back with a very surprised face. 'Mr Badger!' he said.

This was a wonderful thing indeed, for the Badger to come and visit them. He came into the room and stood looking at them, very seriously. The Rat dropped his egg-spoon, and sat open-mouthed.

'The hour has come!' said the Badger at last.

'What hour?' asked the Rat worriedly, looking at the clock on the wall.

'*Whose* hour, you mean,' replied the Badger. 'Why, Toad's hour! The hour of Toad! I said I would teach him a lesson when the summer came, and I'm going to begin today.'

'Toad's hour, of course!' cried the Mole. 'I remember now. *We'll* teach him to be a sensible Toad!'

'I learnt last night,' continued the Badger, 'that another new and very fast motor-car has just arrived at Toad Hall. You two must come with me immediately, and we will save Toad from this madness.'

'Right!' cried the Rat, jumping up. 'Let's go at once.'

When they reached Toad Hall, they saw the new motor-car in front of the house. It was long, shiny, and bright red – Toad's favourite colour. Then Toad himself came down the steps in an enormous overcoat, hat and driving-goggles.

'Hello, you fellows!' Toad called. 'Come for a drive. You're just in time to . . . to . . .'

He saw his friends' serious faces and stopped.

The Badger walked up the steps. 'Come inside the house, Toad,' he said. 'We have to talk to you.'

The three of them took Toad inside and shut the door.

'Now,' the Badger said to Toad, 'first of all, take off those silly driving-clothes.'

'Take off those silly driving-clothes,' said the Badger.

'No, I won't!' replied Toad. 'What is the meaning of this? Explain yourself at once!'

'Take his things off, you two,' ordered the Badger.

It wasn't easy to do. The Rat had to sit on Toad, while the Mole pulled off his overcoat, hat and goggles. And Toad called them some very unpleasant names while this was going on. But when he stood up again, he seemed more like himself, the Toad that they had always known.

'You knew this would happen one day, Toad,' explained

the Badger. 'We've warned you so many times, and you haven't listened. You're spending all your money, you're always in trouble with the police, and you drive like a madman. You will come with me into the next room, and there you will hear some facts about yourself. And you will come out a different Toad.'

He took Toad into a room off the hall and closed the door. The Rat shook his head.

'We won't save Toad by just *talking* to him,' he said. 'He'll *say* anything – and then just go and do what he likes.'

After about an hour the door opened, and a very sad and sorry Toad came out, followed by the Badger.

'My friends,' said the Badger, looking pleased, 'I am happy to tell you that Toad now realizes how silly he has been. He has promised never to get into a motor-car again.'

'That is very good news,' said the Mole seriously.

'Very good indeed,' the Rat said, watching Toad's face carefully.

'Now, Toad,' continued the Badger, 'I'd like you to repeat your promise in front of your friends.'

There was a long, long silence.

'No!' said Toad suddenly. 'No, I won't. I'm *not* sorry, and I haven't been silly at all. It was all wonderful! And I won't promise anything!'

'What?' cried the Badger. 'But in there you told me—'

'Yes, yes, I know,' said Toad quickly. 'You argue so beautifully, dear Badger, and I can't stop myself agreeing with you. But I've been thinking about it. I love driving, I'm a wonderful driver, and I promise you I'll go on driving for ever! Poop-poop!'

'I told you so, didn't I?' the Rat said to the Mole.

'Very well,' said the Badger. 'If you won't listen to reason, we'll have to try another way. We're going to stay with you in your house until you become sensible. Take him upstairs, you two, and lock him in his bedroom.'

So Toad, fighting and shouting, was pulled upstairs by his two friends.

'It's for your own good, Toady, you know,' said the Rat kindly. 'We'll all have good times together again soon, when this – this madness has passed.'

'We'll take good care of you, Toad,' added the Mole. 'No more trouble with the police. No more crashes, and weeks in hospital.'

Then began a very tiring few weeks for the three friends. Day and night they guarded Toad, and one of them was always with him. They talked to him and tried to amuse him, hoping that he would forget his motor-car madness.

But Toad did not seem to get better. He often put the bedroom chairs together to look like a motor-car. Then he sat in the front one and pretended to drive, making terrible engine noises all the time. His friends tried to interest him in other things, but Toad just became sad and silent.

One day the Rat was the guard for the morning. He went upstairs and found Toad still in bed. 'How are you today, old fellow?' he asked brightly.

A sad whisper came from the bed. 'Thank you so much, dear Ratty! But how are *you*, and the excellent Mole, and dear old Badger?'

'Fine, fine,' replied the Rat. 'Badger and Mole,' he added, perhaps not very sensibly, 'have gone out for a run round. They'll be out until lunch-time, so you and I will spend a pleasant morning together.'

'I don't want you to trouble yourself about me,' Toad said, in a sad little voice. 'I was wondering if you would go down to the village and fetch the doctor. But no, it's not important. It's probably too late by now.'

'Are you feeling ill, Toad? What's the matter?'

'I don't know...I think my heart...But you mustn't be sad, Ratty. Dear, kind friend . . . I have enjoyed knowing you so much . . . hate to say goodbye . . .' Toad's whisper became slower and slower, and then stopped.

The Rat felt very worried. Toad lay so still and quiet – perhaps he really was ill. The Rat wished that the other two

Toad lay so still and quiet.

were not so far away. What should he do? He looked again at the still and silent Toad, and decided that he must get the doctor at once. He hurried out, carefully locking the door behind him, and ran off to the village as fast as he could.

When Toad heard the front door bang, he jumped out of bed, laughing loudly. He quickly put on his best suit and filled his pockets with money. Then he took the sheets off the bed, tied them together, and in minutes he had climbed down from the bedroom window and was running across the garden towards the fields.

Toad took the sheets off the bed and tied them together.

A few hours later he was a long way from home. As he walked happily along the road, he felt very pleased with himself. 'A clever piece of work, that was!' he boasted to the trees and the fields. 'Poor old Ratty! A good fellow, but not very intelligent. Badger will be so angry with him!'

Soon he came to a small town and decided to have lunch in the pub there. He was very hungry after his long walk. Halfway through his meal, he heard a sound that he knew very well indeed. Poop-poop! The car stopped outside and the people in it came into the pub to have lunch.

Shaking with excitement, Toad paid his bill and hurried out. He walked slowly round the car, looking at it lovingly. Everybody was having lunch and the street was empty.

'I wonder,' Toad said to himself, 'I wonder if this kind of car *starts* easily?'

It started very easily, and Toad found himself in the driver's seat. He did not know how it happened, but a minute later he was driving out of the town, forgetting right and wrong, forgetting everything except this wonderful, beautiful madness.

Faster and faster he drove, singing and laughing, as the car ate up the miles. Once again he knew that he was Toad – Toad the dreamer, Toad the adventurer, Toad the terror of the open road!

'You are a dangerous criminal,' said the Judge. 'You stole a valuable motor-car, and you drove like a madman. It's surprising that you didn't kill somebody. And finally, you were very rude indeed to the police when they arrested you.

Faster and faster Toad drove, singing and laughing.

Because of all this, I am sending you to prison for twenty years. Guards! Take the prisoner away!'

And so, shouting and crying, Toad was taken away. He was taken to an old dark castle, pushed into the smallest and darkest room below the ground, and the door was locked behind him.

6

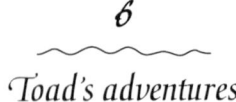

Toad's adventures

For weeks Toad refused to eat. He lay on the floor of his prison and cried and cried. 'This is the end of everything,' he said miserably. 'I shall never again be a popular and good-looking

Toad, a rich and important Toad, a free and happy Toad. All my friends will forget even the name of Toad!'

But the keeper of the prison had a daughter, and she had a very kind heart. She often came to visit Toad, bringing him nice things to eat, and hot drinks. She asked him questions about his home and his old life, and because Toad loved to talk about himself, it wasn't long before he began to sit up and answer her questions. He also realized how hungry he was, and so he ate and drank the things that she brought. And after a few days of this kindness, Toad was as loud and boastful as he had always been.

One morning the girl seemed very serious. 'Listen, Toad,' she said, 'I have an aunt who is a washerwoman.'

'You mustn't worry about it,' said the Toad kindly. 'I have several aunts who *ought* to be washerwomen.'

'Don't talk so much, Toad,' said the girl. 'Now listen, I think I have a plan.' And here she whispered in the Toad's ear.

'What?' cried Toad. 'Me – dress as an old washerwoman? Impossible!'

'All right then,' said the girl crossly. 'You can stay in prison for the next twenty years, you ungrateful animal!'

'No, no,' said Toad quickly. 'You are a good, kind, clever girl, and I am just a stupid toad. I shall be very happy indeed to meet your excellent aunt.'

The next evening a little business was done in the Toad's prison. Several gold coins left the Toad's pocket and disappeared into the washerwoman's purse. Soon afterwards Toad began to climb up the stairs towards the castle entrance. He was wearing an old cotton dress and a black bonnet, and carrying a large basket of washing. And his heart was beating very fast indeed.

Toad began to climb up the stairs towards the castle entrance.

He passed the guards, who called out a friendly 'goodnight' to him, and soon Toad was walking through the streets of the town. He was free! Wild with excitement, he found his way to the railway station – and then came the first problem. He had no money to buy a ticket. His wallet, his keys, his watch – everything was in the pockets of his coat, lying on the prison floor.

He had to get away from this town as quickly as he could. But how could he do it? He walked along beside one of the trains until he came to the engine. Then he stood there, crying and looking up at the engine-driver.

'Hey!' called the driver. 'What's the matter, old lady?'

'Oh, sir!' said Toad. 'I'm a poor unhappy washerwoman, and I've lost all my money, and I *must* get home tonight.'

'Come on, then,' said the engine-driver kindly. 'Jump up, and you can have a free ride. But don't tell anyone!'

So far everything was going well for Toad. The train hurried through the night, taking him away from the hateful prison. But Toad's luck didn't last for long.

There came a moment when the engine-driver put his head out of the window and looked back.

'That's strange,' he said. 'There's a train behind us, coming up very fast. I can see it in the moonlight. I think they're chasing us! I wonder what…' And then the engine-driver gave Toad a long hard look.

So Toad had to tell the true story of his crime and his escape. The engine-driver looked very serious. He thought for a bit, then said, 'I don't like policemen telling me what to do. And I don't like to see an animal crying. So cheer up, Toad! This is what we'll do. In a mile or two the train goes through a wood. I'll slow down there, and you'll be able to jump off the train and get away in the dark.'

Half an hour later both trains had disappeared into the night, and Toad was hiding under some dead leaves in the middle of a strange wood. There, he fell asleep and didn't open his eyes again until early morning. He woke up cold and hungry – but still free!

45

His next adventure was with a barge on a canal. He had walked out of the wood and found a road, which after a while began to run along the side of a canal. Toad liked the idea of getting a free ride, so when he saw the barge coming along the canal, he quickly jumped from the canal bank on to the end of the barge. Then the barge-woman turned and saw him. Toad was ready with his story.

'I'm a poor unhappy washerwoman,' he began.

But the barge-woman, Toad quickly discovered, was a most unpleasant person. She came up to Toad and looked hard at his face under his bonnet. 'Washerwoman indeed! You're a fat lazy little toad, that's what you are!' she said rudely. 'Get off my barge!' And she actually pushed Toad off the barge into the canal.

Toad swam to the bank and climbed out. He was wildly angry. How could he punish this rude and terrible person? Then he saw the horse which was pulling the barge, and an idea came to him.

Two minutes later he was riding the horse across the fields away from the canal. Behind him, the barge-woman was shouting and screaming angrily. Toad rode on, laughing at his own great cleverness.

Later that morning he met a man with a caravan, who was cooking over a fire in a field. Toad sold him the barge-woman's horse for a good price and a hot breakfast. He ate and ate until he was almost too full to move. But he still had a long way to go to get home, so he got up and went on. The sun was shining brightly, his clothes were dry again, and the new

The barge-woman actually pushed Toad into the canal.

coins made a pleasant sound in his pocket. He took off the bonnet, which was too hot, and began to think about all his adventures and escapes.

'Ho, ho!' he said to himself. 'What a clever Toad I am! How brave! How intelligent! No problem is too difficult for Toad!' He began to sing a song about himself as he walked along, although there was no one to hear it. It was perhaps the most boastful song that any animal ever sang.

> *If there's a need the world to save,*
> *Then send for Mr Toad!*
> *There's none so clever, none so brave,*
> *As famous Mr Toad!*

There was a lot more of it, and it got more and more boastful as it went on.

He came to a road and began to walk along it, hoping for another free ride. After a time he saw a small cloud of dust coming up the road behind him, and he heard the noise, that beautiful noise, of a motor-car. He stood in the middle of the road and when the car saw him, it began to slow down.

And then a terrible thing happened. Toad recognized the car and the people in it. And what is worse, the people recognized Toad.

'It's the car thief!' they shouted. 'The criminal who has escaped from prison! Stop him! Catch him!'

Toad turned and ran. He picked up his skirts and ran faster than he had ever run in his life. But the people from the car were now running after him, shouting and screaming at him to stop. They chased him through a wood, across fields, up a hill, and down into a valley. Once Toad looked back and saw that two policemen had joined the chase. He tried to run even faster, but he was a fat animal and his legs were short, and the people were catching up with him.

On and on he ran. He was now among tall trees, and again he looked behind him. At that moment the land disappeared beneath his feet, and, splash! he found himself in deep water, cold water, fast-moving water. In his terror, he had run straight into a river!

And away the river took him, pushing him along, first on one side, then on the other. The cotton dress tied itself round his legs, trying to pull him under, and Toad had to fight to keep his head above water.

'Oh my!' cried poor Toad. 'I'll never look at another

motor-car for the rest of my life!'

At last he managed to catch hold of some water plants by the river bank. He held on, too tired to pull himself out of the water. Then he saw something bright in a dark hole in the bank. It moved towards him, and became a face.

Brown and small, with whiskers.

It was the Water Rat!

7

Return to Toad Hall

The Rat got hold of Toad's neck, pulled him out of the water, and took him into his hall.

'Oh Ratty!' cried Toad. 'I've done so many wonderful things since I last saw you! The dangers that I've been in! I was put in prison – escaped, of course! Pushed into a canal – swam safely away! Stole a horse – sold it for a lot of money! Oh, I *am* a clever Toad, and—'

'Toad,' said the Water Rat, very seriously, 'stop boasting! Go upstairs at once, wash yourself, and put on some of my clothes. I've never seen anything as wet and dirty as you are.'

Toad went upstairs a little crossly, but he was pleased to get out of the washerwoman's dress. He came down very clean and tidy, and ready to tell the Rat all about his adventures – how clever, how brave, how successful he had been. The Rat gave him lunch, and listened, unsmiling, while Toad talked and talked and talked. When at last he finished, the Rat looked up.

'I have to tell you, Toad,' he said slowly, 'that I feel ashamed – yes, ashamed, to have a criminal, an escaped prisoner, for my friend. Can't you see that none of this is exciting or amusing?'

There was a little silence. Then Toad said sadly, 'You're right, Ratty. Of course you are. How silly and boastful I have been! I shall become a quiet, sensible Toad from now on. In a while I'll walk down to Toad Hall and—'

'Walk down to Toad Hall?' cried the Rat. 'What are you talking about? Haven't you *heard*?'

'Heard what?' said Toad, looking frightened. 'Quick, Ratty, tell me! What haven't I heard?'

'About the Wild Wooders!' cried the Rat. 'The Stoats and the Weasels and the Ferrets – they've taken Toad Hall! When you were sent to prison, they came out of the Wild Wood one dark night and broke into the Hall. They've been living there ever since – eating your food, drinking your drink, giving wild parties. They've got guns and knives and sticks, and they keep guards round the house night and day. They say they're going to stay there for ever.'

At first Toad couldn't believe it. But he had gone up to Toad Hall, and two ferrets in the garden had laughed at him, and the stoats who were guarding the walls had shot at him. Toad dropped flat in the road and the bullet passed over his head. He went back, very unhappy, to the Water Rat.

That night there was a meeting in the Rat's house. The Mole

The ferrets laughed at him, and the stoats shot at him.

and the Badger came, to talk about plans to take back Toad Hall from the Wild Wooders.

When they came in and saw Toad, the Badger shook his head sadly. 'Poor Toad! This is not a happy home-coming for you.'

But the Mole was very pleased to see him. 'Here's old Toad!' he cried. 'How did you manage to escape from prison? It was very clever of you to do that.'

'Clever?' said Toad. 'Well, I don't want to boast, Mole. I'll tell you all about it and *you* can decide if—'

'Toad, do be quiet, please!' said the Rat. 'We need to discuss plans. I think I know the best way for Toad to—'

'No, you don't!' said the Mole. 'I know what Toad should do. He should—'

'Well, I'm not going to!' cried Toad, getting excited. 'I'm not taking orders from you fellows! It's my house that we're talking about and—'

51

By now they were almost shouting at each other, when suddenly a deep low voice came from an armchair.

'Be quiet at once, all of you!' said the Badger. 'And listen. The Mole and I have been watching Toad Hall. The stoats, with their guns, are on guard all round the walls, and they're very good guards too. We can't attack the place from outside. They're too strong for us.'

'Then there's no hope,' cried Toad miserably. 'I shall go and join the army or something, and never see my dear Toad Hall again!'

'Cheer up, Toady,' said the Badger, 'because now I'm going to tell you a very great secret.'

Toad sat up, interested. He loved secrets, although he could never keep them.

'There – is – an – underground – tunnel,' said the Badger slowly, 'which goes from the river bank near here, right up into the middle of Toad Hall.'

'Don't be silly, Badger!' cried Toad. 'Of course there isn't! I know Toad Hall, inside and outside, and—'

'My young friend,' said the Badger calmly, 'your father – who was a great friend of mine – told me many things that he didn't tell *you*. "Don't tell my son about this tunnel," he said to me. "He's a good boy, but he talks far too much." '

Toad opened his mouth to argue, and then decided not to.

'I asked Otter,' continued the Badger, 'to do some spy work for us. He pretended to be a gardener and went to the back door of the Hall, asking for work. During the conversation he learnt that tomorrow night there will be a big birthday party –

the Chief Weasel's, I think – in the dining-hall. All the weasels will be there, eating and drinking and laughing, and making a lot of noise.'

'But the stoats will still be on guard on the walls,' said the Rat.

'True,' agreed the Badger. 'But the weasels, you see, know that, so they won't have any guns or sticks with them at the party. And the tunnel comes up into that little room right next to the dining-hall. We only have to—'

'—run into the dining-hall—' cried the Mole.

'—with our guns and sticks and knives—' shouted the Rat.

'—and chase them and beat them and hit them!' cried the Toad, greatly excited. He ran round and round the room, jumping over the chairs.

'Very well, then,' said the Badger, sitting back comfortably and opening his newspaper. 'That is the plan, and there's nothing more for you to argue about.'

All the next day the Rat hurried about, getting the guns and the knives and the sticks ready. Once the Badger lifted his head from the newspaper.

'We shan't need guns or knives, Ratty,' he said. 'We four, with our sticks, will clear the dining-hall in five minutes. I could do it by myself.'

'Better to be safe than sorry,' said the Rat.

At last the evening came, and the four friends went quietly along the river bank to find the entrance to the secret tunnel. Toad, of course, managed to fall in the river and his friends had to pull him out. The tunnel was cold, and wet, and dark, and narrow. Poor Toad got frightened and ran into the Rat by mistake, who then nearly knocked the Mole over. All this made a lot of noise, and the Badger, who was in front with the lantern, turned round.

'If Toad can't keep quiet,' he whispered angrily, 'I'll leave him here alone in the dark!'

After that, the Toad kept very quiet.

They could hear the noise of the party while they were still underground. Silently, they pushed open the door in the roof of the tunnel, and climbed up into the small room next to the dining-hall. Now they could hear one of the weasels singing a very rude song about Toad the car-thief.

'Just wait until I get my hands on him!' Toad whispered angrily, showing his teeth.

'Right, boys!' said the Badger, looking round at his friends. 'The hour has come! Follow me!'

And they crashed through the door into the dining-hall.

What a battle it was!

What a battle it was! How the four friends roared as they ran through the hall! What screams of fear came from the surprised weasels and ferrets! Tables and chairs were knocked over, plates and glasses went crashing to the floor. Up and down went the four friends, shouting and roaring, and their sticks whistled through the air. There were only four of them, but they seemed enormous to the weasels and the ferrets. The Wild Wooders ran in terror, escaping through the doors and windows, and even up the chimneys – anywhere to get away from those terrible sticks.

In five minutes the room was cleared. The stoats outside, the four friends discovered later, had gone too. They were already frightened by the noise of battle from the hall, so when the weasels and the ferrets started running out in terror, the stoats dropped their guns and ran back to the Wild Wood. In fact, after that night there was no more trouble from the Wild Wooders for a long time. And when any of them met the

Badger and his friends out for a walk, they were very polite indeed.

Back in Toad Hall, there was a lot of tidying up to do after the battle. At last it was all done, and the four friends, tired but happy, went upstairs to bed.

'And now,' said the Badger, after breakfast the next morning, 'we must have a Victory Party. Toad, you must write and invite all our friends for tonight.'

'What – me do all the work?' said Toad crossly. 'Why . . .' He suddenly stopped, then said, 'Yes, of course. I'll do everything. I'll plan the party, and the singing and—'

'Oh no,' said the Rat. 'You're not going to sing any of your songs.'

'Not just one *little* song?' asked Toad miserably.

'No, Toady. You know very well that your songs are all about you and how clever you are. They're just one long boast!'

'Come on now, Toad,' said the Badger kindly. 'You know that you have to change your ways and become a sensible animal. Why not begin now? What better moment could there be, on your return to Toad Hall?'

Toad looked at his three friends' serious faces. For a long while he seemed to be thinking deeply. At last he spoke. 'My friends, you are right,' he said sadly. 'And I am wrong. From today, I will be a very different Toad. You will never be ashamed of me again.'

The party was a great success. Everyone wanted to hear about the battle, and there was a lot of noisy talking and laughing. But Toad was not at all noisy. He moved quietly round the room, making sure that everyone had enough to eat and drink. He said very little about the battle, only, 'Oh, it was Badger's clever plan. And the Mole and the Rat did all the hard fighting.'

Toad moved quietly round the room.

His three friends watched him with their mouths open in surprise – which pleased Toad very much. Towards the end of the evening, some of the younger animals started banging on the table and shouting, 'Toad! Song! Mr Toad's Song!' But Toad only shook his head gently, and immediately began a quiet conversation with Otter, asking in an interested voice about his children.

He was indeed a different Toad!

GLOSSARY

attack *(v)* to begin fighting or trying to hurt someone

boast *(v)* to say that everything you are and everything you do is the best in the world

bother a word you say when you are a little angry

dining-hall a large room where meals are eaten

enormous very big

fellow a friendly word for a man (here, a male animal)

guard *(n)* someone who watches a prisoner or keeps a building safe

judge a person who decides if a someone is a criminal or not

madness sickness in the mind

mess about to play around, to do pleasant, silly, unimportant things

patter *(v)* to make quick, light sounds (like the sound of rain falling or small feet running)

pleasant nice, enjoyable, pleasing

roar *(v)* to make a long, loud, deep sound

rude not polite

silly not sensible or serious; a little stupid

terror very great fear

victory winning a battle or a fight

washerwoman a woman whose work is washing other people's clothes

whisper *(v)* to speak very softly and quietly

whistle *(v)* to make a sound by blowing through nearly closed lips

The Wind in the Willows

ACTIVITIES

Before Reading

Read the back cover of the book, and the story introduction on the first page. How much do you know now about this story? Choose T (true) or F (false) for each sentence.

1 The Mole is used to life on the river. T/F
2 The Water Rat enjoys life on the river. T/F
3 The Mole and the Rat spend the summer together. T/F
4 Mr Toad is a sensible person. T/F
5 Mr Toad is very interested in boats. T/F
6 Mr Toad has a very good opinion of himself. T/F

2 What can you guess about this story? Choose endings for these sentences (you can choose more than one).

1 *The Wind in the Willows* is a story . . .
   a) about an unreal world where strange things happen.
   b) about animals who behave like people.
   c) about how animals and people can live together.
   d) which ends sadly, with a death.
   e) which ends happily, with a party.
2 When Toad goes crazy about motor-cars, . . .
   a) he buys several cars and crashes them all.
   b) he has a bad accident and kills one of his friends.
   c) his friends enjoy going for drives with him.
   d) his friends get cross and try to stop him driving.
   e) he steals a car and is sent to prison.

ACTIVITIES

While Reading

Read Chapters 1 and 2. Choose the best question-word for these questions, and then answer them.

What / Who

1 . . . had the Mole never seen before in his life?
2 . . . came to join the Rat and the Mole at their lunch party?
3 . . . saw the friends, but didn't join the lunch party?
4 . . . did the friends see rowing very badly up the river?
5 . . . had yellow and green sides, and red wheels?
6 . . . thought that the travelling life would be a great adventure?
7 . . . came past the friends on the road in a storm of noise and wind and dust?
8 . . . did Toad do the day after the accident with the caravan?

Before you read Chapter 3 (*The Wild Wood*), can you guess what happens? Choose names to complete these sentences.

the Rat / the Mole / Toad / the Badger / the Otter

1 _____ goes for a walk in the Wild Wood and gets very frightened.
2 _____ goes to look for him, but then they both get lost.
3 In the end they find their way to _____'s house.
4 _____ also goes to look for them in the wood.

Read Chapters 3 and 4. Are these sentences true (T) or false (F)? Rewrite the false sentences with the correct information.

1 The Badger, who lived near the Rat's home, loved parties.
2 The Rat did not really like going into the Wild Wood.
3 In the Wild Wood the Mole was chased by the weasels, stoats, and ferrets, and he became very frightened.
4 The Rat knew the Mole had gone out, but he did nothing.
5 In the dark the Rat fell over a rock and cut himself.
6 The Badger gave the Mole and the Rat a warm welcome.
7 Toad was a careful driver and had not had any crashes.
8 The friends agreed to do something about Toad at once.
9 The Otter was not afraid of anybody in the Wild Wood.
10 The Badger and the Mole thought it was safer and more comfortable to live underground, and the Rat agreed.

Before you read Chapter 5 (*A lesson for Mr Toad*), what can you guess about the lesson? Choose some of these answers.

The lesson for Mr Toad will be to teach him . . .

1 to drive a car safely.
2 to row a boat well.
3 to forget about motor-cars.
4 not to be boastful.
5 to be a sensible fellow.
6 to spend less money.

Read Chapters 5 and 6. Choose the best question-word for these questions, and then answer them.

How / What / Where
1 . . . made the Rat drop his egg-spoon at breakfast one day?
2 . . . did the three friends go that morning?

3 ... did they see when they got there?
4 ... did the Rat and the Mole do to Toad?
5 ... did the friends lock Toad?
6 ... did Toad escape from his house?
7 ... did Toad do after his lunch in a pub?
8 ... did Toad escape from prison?
9 ... did Toad sleep the first night after his escape?
10 ... did Toad get some money and a hot breakfast?
11 ... happened when Toad was chased by the people from the car?
12 ... did the river take Toad?

Before you read Chapter 7 (*Return to Toad Hall*), can you guess how the story ends? Choose some of these ideas.

1 Toad boasts about his escape and his adventures.
2 Toad's friends think he should go back to prison.
3 Toad cannot go home because Toad Hall has burnt down.
4 The Weasels, Stoats, and Ferrets have taken Toad Hall.
5 Toad goes to live with the Rat.
6 Toad goes to live with the Badger.
7 Toad and his friends fight a battle to take Toad Hall back.
8 Toad promises to change his ways and become sensible.

Read Chapter 7. How many of your guesses were right? Check your answers, and then talk about this question.

Has Toad really changed into a sensible person? Will he never be boastful or do silly things again? What do *you* think?

After Reading

1 **Match these halves of sentences about Toad's adventures, and complete them with the right names. (You will need some names more than once, and for some gaps you will need more than one name.)**

the Badger / the Rat / the Mole / the barge-woman / the judge / the prison-keeper's daughter / the engine-driver

1 When _____ travelled with Toad in his caravan, . . .

2 _____ wanted to stop Toad driving motor-cars, . . .

3 One morning Toad pretended to be very ill, . . .

4 While _____ was out, fetching the doctor, . . .

5 _____ sent Toad to prison for twenty years . . .

6 In prison Toad became friendly with _____, . . .

7 _____ didn't like to see an animal cry, . . .

8 _____ pushed Toad into the canal . . .

9 Toad climbed out of the window and escaped.

10 so he let Toad jump off the train and escape.

11 they had to do all the work because Toad was so lazy.

12 because she saw that he was a fat lazy little toad, not a poor washerwoman at all.

13 who made a plan for him to escape as a washerwoman.

14 and asked _____ to fetch a doctor from the village.

15 so they kept Toad a prisoner in his bedroom.

16 because Toad stole a motor-car and drove like a madman.

2 **Here is Toad, talking about his adventures, but, as usual, he is boasting and most of what he says is not true. How would his friends rewrite the passage to make it a true story?**

'When they sent me to prison, I was very brave and I didn't cry at all. Nobody was kind to me, and I had only bread and water. I escaped without any help from anybody. I wore a guard's clothes and jumped out of a window. Then I walked all through the night. In the morning I met a barge-woman, who said I was very good-looking. She gave me her horse, which I gave away later to a poor woman.'

3 **Here are Rat and Mole, telling Badger about their adventure in the Wild Wood. Decide who is speaking each time (Rat or Mole), and put their story in the right order. Begin with number 3.**

1 _____ 'And we did, but I thought Ratty was going crazy!'

2 _____ 'I was pleased to see him, too! But later, when we started walking home, we got lost in the snow.'

3 _____ 'I was very silly. I went out by myself to walk in the Wild Wood while Ratty was sleeping by the fire.'

4 _____ 'And then we found your front door. Moly was so surprised!'

5 _____ 'Ratty found me hiding in an old tree. I was so pleased to see him, Mr Badger, you can't imagine!'

6 _____ 'So I told Moly we had to start digging at once!'

7 _____ 'Yes, and when I woke up, I realized where Moly had gone, and followed him at once.'

8 _____ 'Luckily, I fell over your door-scraper . . .'

4 There are 26 words (four letters or longer) from the story in this word search. Find the words, and draw lines through them. Words go from left to right, and from top to bottom.

I	H	E	D	G	E	H	O	G	M	T	O	A	D
G	S	I	L	L	Y	O	T	U	N	N	E	L	I
W	N	G	W	I	L	D	T	T	W	O	T	C	F
H	S	Q	U	I	R	R	E	L	E	H	O	L	E
I	T	E	B	L	U	A	R	B	A	D	G	E	R
S	O	L	A	Y	D	B	O	A	S	T	O	V	R
P	A	U	N	A	E	B	M	R	E	V	E	E	E
E	T	R	K	Y	G	I	O	G	L	R	E	R	T
R	A	W	H	I	S	T	L	E	W	O	O	D	T
C	A	R	A	V	A	N	E	S	R	I	V	E	R
E	C	C	A	N	A	L	R	E	B	O	A	T	T

1 How many of the words are the names of animals?

2 Which important animal from the story is missing?

3 Which words are the opposites of these three words?

POLITE   SHOUT   SENSIBLE

5 Now write down all the letters in the word search that don't have a line through them. Begin with the first line, and go across each line to the end. You should have 32 letters, which will make a sentence of 9 words. What is the sentence?

1 Who said this to Toad, and what was he talking about?

2 Why didn't Toad already know about it?

3 How did this thing help Toad?

6 Perhaps this is what some of the characters in the story were thinking. Who are they, and what is happening in the story at this moment?

  1 'What's that? Surely it can't be my front door bell at this time of night? Yes, it is! And there's someone banging on the door too. They're going to hear a few angry words when I get up there!'

  2 'She's a clever girl, my niece. With all these gold coins I can now buy myself a nice new cotton dress and a new bonnet. I never liked that old black bonnet much. Ooh, he did look funny in it!'

  3 'Oh dear! I can see he really wants to go on this journey – he thinks it will be an exciting adventure. I'll have to agree, I suppose. But I'd much prefer to be on the river, messing about in a boat . . .'

  4 'Yes, I can see they're all watching me. They look so surprised – they just can't believe that I've become sensible at last! Ah, there's Otter. I'll go and talk to him now, ask him about his children . . .'

  5 'I'm *sure* I could do it – it looks so easy. Why won't he let me try? I don't see the need to have lessons first. Perhaps I'll just jump up and take the oars for a minute . . .'

7 Which character did you like best in the story, and which did you like least? Write a few lines to explain why.

ABOUT THE AUTHOR

Kenneth Grahame was born in 1859 in Edinburgh, Scotland. As a child he did not have a very happy life. His mother died when he was five, and his father sent him and his sister and two brothers south to England, to live with their grandmother. She was not a kind woman, but she lived in a village by the river Thames, and Kenneth spent many happy days exploring the river. He went to school in Oxford, and wanted to go to the university there, but his family was not rich enough to pay for his studies. Instead, he went to London and took a job with the Bank of England, where he worked for nearly thirty years.

In London he began to write, and had his first great success with two books of stories about children, *The Golden Age* (1895) and *Dream Days* (1898). His next and most famous book, The *Wind in the Willows*, began as bedtime stories for his young son Alastair, who was called Mouse. It finally appeared as a book in 1908, but after this, Grahame wrote almost nothing. Sadly, his son Alastair died as a young man, and Grahame and his wife lived rather strange, lonely lives. He died in 1932, not far from the river Thames that he loved so much.

The Wind in the Willows has become a much-loved classic of children's literature. It is not really about animals, but about people – certain kinds of English gentlemen of those times. The story has been a children's musical play, *Toad of Toad Hall*, and some famous artists have drawn illustrations for it. One artist, E. H. Shepard, went to see Grahame to talk about the drawings he planned to do. Grahame, now an old man, listened patiently, and then said: 'I love these little people, be kind to them.'

OXFORD BOOKWORMS LIBRARY

Classics • Crime & Mystery • Factfiles • Fantasy & Horror
Human Interest • Playscripts • Thriller & Adventure
True Stories • World Stories

The OXFORD BOOKWORMS LIBRARY provides enjoyable reading in English, with a wide range of classic and modern fiction, non-fiction, and plays. It includes original and adapted texts in seven carefully graded language stages, which take learners from beginner to advanced level. An overview is given on the next pages.

All Stage 1 titles are available as audio recordings, as well as over eighty other titles from Starter to Stage 6. All Starters and many titles at Stages 1 to 4 are specially recommended for younger learners. Every Bookworm is illustrated, and Starters and Factfiles have full-colour illustrations.

The OXFORD BOOKWORMS LIBRARY also offers extensive support. Each book contains an introduction to the story, notes about the author, a glossary, and activities. Additional resources include tests and worksheets, and answers for these and for the activities in the books. There is advice on running a class library, using audio recordings, and the many ways of using Oxford Bookworms in reading programmes. Resource materials are available on the website <www.oup.com/bookworms>.

The *Oxford Bookworms Collection* is a series for advanced learners. It consists of volumes of short stories by well-known authors, both classic and modern. Texts are not abridged or adapted in any way, but carefully selected to be accessible to the advanced student.

You can find details and a full list of titles in the *Oxford Bookworms Library Catalogue* and *Oxford English Language Teaching Catalogues*, and on the website <www.oup.com/bookworms>.

THE OXFORD BOOKWORMS LIBRARY
GRADING AND SAMPLE EXTRACTS

STARTER • 250 HEADWORDS

present simple – present continuous – imperative –
can/cannot, must – *going to* (future) – simple gerunds …

Her phone is ringing – but where is it?

Sally gets out of bed and looks in her bag. No phone. She looks under the bed. No phone. Then she looks behind the door. There is her phone. Sally picks up her phone and answers it. *Sally's Phone*

STAGE 1 • 400 HEADWORDS

… past simple – coordination with *and, but, or* –
subordination with *before, after, when, because, so* …

I knew him in Persia. He was a famous builder and I worked with him there. For a time I was his friend, but not for long. When he came to Paris, I came after him – I wanted to watch him. He was a very clever, very dangerous man. *The Phantom of the Opera*

STAGE 2 • 700 HEADWORDS

… present perfect – *will* (future) – *(don't) have to, must not, could* –
comparison of adjectives – simple *if* clauses – past continuous –
tag questions – *ask/tell* + infinitive …

While I was writing these words in my diary, I decided what to do. I must try to escape. I shall try to get down the wall outside. The window is high above the ground, but I have to try. I shall take some of the gold with me – if I escape, perhaps it will be helpful later. *Dracula*

... should, may – present perfect continuous – *used to* – past perfect –
causative – relative clauses – indirect statements ...

Of course, it was most important that no one should see
Colin, Mary, or Dickon entering the secret garden. So Colin
gave orders to the gardeners that they must all keep away
from that part of the garden in future. *The Secret Garden*

... past perfect continuous – passive (simple forms) –
would conditional clauses – indirect questions –
relatives with *where/when* – gerunds after prepositions/phrases ...

I was glad. Now Hyde could not show his face to the world
again. If he did, every honest man in London would be proud
to report him to the police. *Dr Jekyll and Mr Hyde*

... future continuous – future perfect –
passive (modals, continuous forms) –
would have conditional clauses – modals + perfect infinitive ...

If he had spoken Estella's name, I would have hit him. I was so
angry with him, and so depressed about my future, that I could
not eat the breakfast. Instead I went straight to the old house.
Great Expectations

... passive (infinitives, gerunds) – advanced modal meanings –
clauses of concession, condition

When I stepped up to the piano, I was confident. It was as if I
knew that the prodigy side of me really did exist. And when I
started to play, I was so caught up in how lovely I looked that
I didn't worry how I would sound. *The Joy Luck Club*

A Christmas Carol

CHARLES DICKENS

Retold by Clare West

Christmas is humbug, Scrooge says – just a time when you find yourself a year older and not a penny richer. The only thing that matters to Scrooge is business, and making money.

But on Christmas Eve three spirits come to visit him. They take him travelling on the wings of the night to see the shadows of Christmas past, present, and future – and Scrooge learns a lesson that he will never forget.

The Star Zoo

HARRY GILBERT

In our world today a hummingbird is a small, brilliantly coloured bird that lives in the tall trees of tropical forests.

In the far distant future, Hummingbird (Hummy for short) is a girl of sixteen who lives somewhere in the Galaxy, on a planet called Just Like Home. She has the name 'Hummingbird' in big letters on all her clothes, but she has never seen a real hummingbird. She has never seen any living animal or bird at all. The Book of Remembering says that there were once many animals on a planet called Earth, but that was before the Burning, a long, long time ago …

THE WIND IN THE WILLOWS

'Do you know,' the Mole said, 'I've never been in a boat before in all my life.'

'What?' cried the Rat. 'My dear fellow, you haven't lived! Believe me, there is *nothing* – really nothing – nicer than just messing about in boats.'

And so the Mole learns a new way of life with his friend the Water Rat. Long, golden summer days on the river, while the wind whispers its secrets through the willow trees. Life is full of excitement and adventure, and new friends: the Otter and the Badger, and of course, Mr Toad – the famous, the clever, the brave, the wonderful Mr Toad . . .

Well, that's what Toad thinks, but his friends are not so sure. And when he goes crazy about motor-cars, he becomes a very silly, and a very dangerous Toad . . .